DOGGY DEFENDERS

NATIONAL GEOGRAPHIC KiDS

DOLLEY

★ ★ ★

THE FIRE DOG

Lisa M. Gerry
Photographs by Lori Epstein

NATIONAL GEOGRAPHIC
WASHINGTON, D.C.

★ ★ ★

Meet DOLLEY!

★ ★ ★

Dolley is a Labrador retriever.

Like most dogs,
she loves getting **snuggles** ...

... and playing **fetch!**

But Dolley is also different from other dogs. She has a job!

Dolley is a **fire dog.**

Dolley's partner is her owner,

Captain Herndon.

★10★

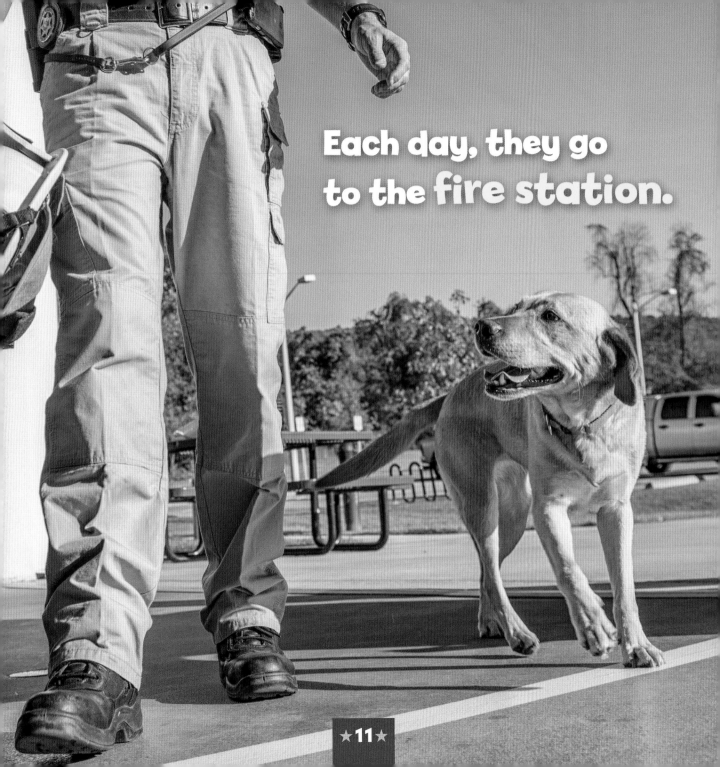

Each day, they go to the **fire station.**

There is a lot of work for the firefighters—and for Dolley, too!

Dolley's job is very important. When there is a fire, she sniffs out what started it.

Dolley can smell a drop of fire-starting liquid

that is smaller than a coin.

Dolley works hard to keep her **super sniffer** in tip-top shape. Captain Herndon helps Dolley practice by hiding scents for her to find.

Is it hidden in this can? Yes! Dolley gets a **tasty reward** for finding the scent.

Sometimes Captain Herndon hides the scent outside, at a special place called a burn house. Then he says to Dolley, "Seek!"

Dolley's off!

She sniffs all around to find what Captain Herndon hid.

Dolley uses her **strong nose** to search up high ... and down low.

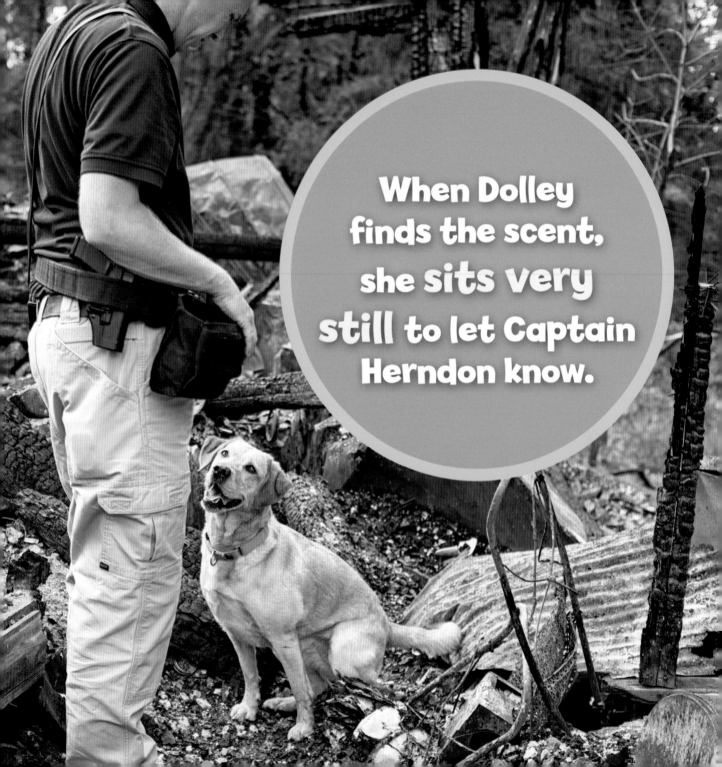

When Dolley finds the scent, she sits very still to let Captain Herndon know.

And now for the yummy part—Dolley gets some kibble as a reward. **Mmm!**

After a fun time practicing, Dolley gets cleaned up. Captain Herndon uses a special tool to wash her paws.

One, two, three, four ... all done!

Next, Dolley helps kids practice fire safety!

Dolley shows kids how to prevent fires and stay safe if there is a fire.

She also teaches them to **stop, drop, and roll!**

Now it's time for Dolley to stop practicing.

Captain Herndon has gotten a call—there is a **real fire!**

When Dolley and Captain Herndon arrive, the other firefighters have put out the flames. It's Dolley's turn to do her job!

Very carefully, Dolley sniffs and sniffs ...

... and **sniffs** and **sniffs.**

Suddenly, she sits down. Dolley has found the cause of the fire! Now the firefighters know where it started. Good job, Dolley!

But all that hard work has made Dolley dirty.

Oh no! Another bath?

Dolley shake, shake, shakes to get dry, and then gets wrapped in a warm, cozy towel.

It's been a long day, and Dolley is ready to go home with Captain Herndon. Now she can **relax** with her family ...

... and play!

Dolley loves her job, but she also loves being an off-duty dog.

At work or at home,
Dolley is always a hero.
Good job, Dolley!

Sweet dreams!

Meet the Team!

Captain Herndon answers questions about Dolley and being a fire investigator.

Q How did you get Dolley?

A I was paired with Dolley through the ATF, the Bureau of Alcohol, Tobacco, Firearms and Explosives. The ATF is a law enforcement agency in the United States' Department of Justice.

Q Who trained Dolley?

A The ATF trained Dolley for 12 weeks.

Squirt

Jimmy

Dolley

Q What do you and Dolley do in your free time?

A Dolley likes to play fetch or relax, though she's usually very busy!

Q What is Dolley's favorite game?

A She loves to swim.

Q What is the best part of being a fire investigator?

A The best part of being a fire investigator for the Loudoun County Fire Marshal's Office is getting to help people who are in need, especially during emergencies.

Dolley's Safety Tips

Dolley is an expert at fire safety—and you can be, too! Follow these tips to help prevent fires, and to know what to do in case of an emergency.

1. Never play with fire, and report those that do to local authorities.

2. Know how to dial 9-1-1 and be able to provide your address.

3. Have a smoke alarm on every floor of your home and one in every bedroom.

4. Change the batteries in your smoke alarms every six months (you can do this when you change your clocks in the spring and fall).

5. Replace your smoke alarms every 10 years.

6. Have an exit plan for emergencies. The plan should include two ways to get outside and a meeting spot. Remember to practice your exit plan often.

7. Consider closing your bedroom door at night to prevent smoke and heat from entering your room if there is an emergency.

8. In case of a fire, check all doors for heat before opening them.

9. During an emergency, never hide—go outside. Once you are outside, stay outside.

10. If your clothes catch fire, remember to stop, drop, and roll.

Since 1888, the National Geographic Society has funded more than 12,000 research, exploration, and preservation projects around the world. The Society receives funds from National Geographic Partners, LLC, funded in part by your purchase. A portion of the proceeds from this book supports this vital work. To learn more, visit natgeo.com/info.

For more information, visit nationalgeographic.com, call 1-800-647-5463, or write to the following address:

National Geographic Partners
1145 17th Street N.W.
Washington, D.C. 20036-4688 U.S.A.

Visit us online at nationalgeographic.com/books
For librarians and teachers: ngchildrensbooks.org
More for kids from National Geographic:
natgeokids.com

National Geographic Kids magazine inspires children to explore their world with fun yet educational articles on animals, science, nature, and more. Using fresh story-telling and amazing photography, *Nat Geo Kids* shows kids ages 6 to 14 the fascinating truth about the world—and why they should care.
kids.nationalgeographic.com/subscribe

For information about special discounts for bulk pur-chases, please contact National Geographic Books Special Sales: specialsales@natgeo.com

LOUDOUN COUNTY

For rights or permissions inquiries, please contact National Geographic Books Subsidiary Rights: bookrights@natgeo.com

Designed by Callie Broaddus

The publisher would like to thank Lisa Gerry, author; Lori Epstein, photographer; Paige Towler, project editor; Shannon Hibberd, photo editor; and Dolley, Captain Herndon, Dolley's family, the entire Loudoun County Combined Fire and Rescue System, and Briggs Animal Adoption Center for their support and dedication to their communities.

Hardcover ISBN: 978-1-4263-3299-9
Reinforced library binding ISBN: 978-1-4263-3300-2

Printed in China
19/PPS/1